Poetry

694

1st ed. vg in a yellow
base dj that shows some
soil.

THE IMAGE COLLECTOR VII

The
Image Collector VII

by

Marjorie Duryee

HOUSE OF FALMOUTH, INC.

Portland, Maine

FOR MY AUNT MAME

CONTENTS

THE IMAGE COLLECTOR VII

THE BRETON SAILOR, DROWNED AT SEA

(for R. B. C. O'C.)

There was such a pallor
to the face of the Breton sailor
as he lay there dead
on the foredeck of the fishing vessel
moored to the quay
in the heart of Concarneau,
such a sallow cast to the greenish-grey,
we could hardly take our eyes away.

Yet we didn't want to seem to linger
for fear they'd think us curious.
What else?
Being tourists,
we could hardly share
the sorrow of the villagers gathered there that
Sunday.

Yes, the church bells had been tolling
when the tuna boat with its reddish pink and
orange sails
against the saffron lemon sky
had come sailing up the estuary
with its dreadful burden,
carrying the body of the sailor
drowned a month ago,
wrapped in a shroud of canvas,
just a corner falling off
to reveal his ravaged face
as sallow as the mildewed sail it was covered with.

For the mid-July tempest
blowing up the day before
had forced the sea of its awesome catch,
and the body of the sailor cast up
off the Isles of Glénans
had been found by his fellows
and brought home to rest at last.

Now this Sunday morning,
the townsfolk stood there, in their sorrow,
on the shelving stonework of the inner harbor
      of Concarneau,
the morning sun a pale greying runny yellow,
and the sky and sea a sallow swimmy yellow, too,
and even the air smelled sickly yellow
in the humid heat coming in waves across the bay.

The women stood there in their sorrow,
as the church bells tolled,
their cone-shaped coifs of Irish point lace
as startling white on that grey day
as the whites of staring eyes;
and the men in black felt hats and embroidered
      vests
composed their faces even more severely
as they paid homage to their fellow worker of the sea;
and we felt out of place,
their sorrow was so personal,
as if the death of one of them
could be of no real concern to us.

We didn't talk about it then,
or even later,
and though we were leaving on the morrow
for Paris by way of Laval, Alencon, and Chartres,
little did we know we'd be taking with us
the face of that dead sailor;
indeed, would carry it through the following
    waves of heat
through the narrow streets of Paris,
and take it with us on the train
when we left the first of August for Grenoble,
where we were going to study French.

However, this was the year before the war,
and toward the middle of September,
before Chamberlain made his flight to Munich,
we had gone to London,
where, when we saw the sand bags and the trenches,
we saw and lost the sailor's face
among the faces of the men digging there,
and all the others, greenish-grey,
in restaurants, in the streets and buses;
and while Londoners queued up for gas masks,

we stood in line pushing for a passage home
in the Cunard steamship office;
and one afternoon, the proprietor of a tea shop
    in Cambridge,
letting us borrow his black umbrella
to help us through the rain,
shook his head at the closing of the University.
Just like it was before, he kept telling us.

And then the morning came
when the chambermaid came in and said,
we'll never have another war in our century.
Yes, it's true. Peace with honor.
It says so on the piece of paper.
Yes, they both signed it,
and he's brought it home.
And outside the hotel window,
the placard at the newsstand
danced and sang
with the great black block letters shouting,
EUROPE'S DAY OF JOY.

And in a joy of our own,
relieved that we could stay and wouldn't have
    to hurry home,
we forgot we'd ever come across that Breton
    sailor,
his face so yellow-green
on the deck of the fishing vessel
in the heart of Concarneau
that summer day
all sallow yellow greenish-grey
in the middle of July.

And the men in restaurants, streets and buses
no longer bore the look
of the war they remembered;
and with only five hours notice,
steamship tickets were refunded;
and when the pound went up, the banker
    said to us,
not much to pay for peace, surely.

And then when they stopped digging trenches in
    Hyde Park,
it seemed a real good sign;
and so we wrote to everyone we knew
to show off our new return address,
Half Moon Chambers, Half Moon Street,
(with skylight and coal fireplace),
a neat address, we thought, half-whimsical,
close to Shepherd Market,
and so much else, too.

ADVICE FROM VENCE

In Vence, once,
in the vestibule of a church,
a definition by the newsstand;
    "Any papers taken
    even for a little time
    and not paid for
    are stolen."

In the Place du Peyra,
in the old part of town,
a prohibition posted:
    "It is forbidden
    to wash your linen
    or vegetables
    in the fountain."

And out on the Avenue Henri Matisse,
in the Dominican Chapel of the Rosary,
where, like the soft notes of an organ,
the colors come and go,
a summation by the master:
    "The result of a life of work."

THE WANDERER

So many times I missed the door of heaven
and didn't even know
until someone told me later,
that when I passed the doorway in the
    Casbah in Tangiers,
so palely white
with its trim of poignant iris blue,
I thought,
oh no, not this one, too.

But something drove me onward
and I pursued my way
on the narrow ill-lit path
going round the corner,
sure that when I came upon another doorway,
perhaps this time in Cadiz,
just as palely white
with a trim of dark blue iris blue,
I would at least look twice
to see if this would do.

That is if in the interim
someone else had not kindly said
from a doorway say pink and ochre red
with a twist of sky-blue blue,
O, it's you,
and then pulling the beaded curtain aside,
step in, won't you?
Well, why don't you?

SUNDAY PASEO

Flotillas of families
flow and float along the *avenidas,*
sailing slowly proudly
in the wash of shadows from the palm trees; *plane*
the shade-sheltered tables full of savorers
of many kinds of teas,
and passers-by like these;

acacia blossoms on the sidewalk
seem a cool occasional yellow snow,
a welcome feel of snow, this hot mid-August Sunday;
and a solitary and a couple
sip their sugared lemonades,
read the ABC and other morning papers,
and regard a certain family,
in full regalia,
making their *paseo*
on this candy holiday
sweetened by the sweat of a drudging week of work.

Two girls in organdy and muslin,
buoyed with starch, white gloves on,
and three boys in fresh white sailor suits,
hats with streamers,
hold balloons and red and yellow flags,
and march along, following in the wake
their parents make,

the patriarch in stiff black suit,
his wife in silken blouse and rustly skirt;
and on this Sunday stroll through the yellow cool
and waves of heat,

10

they push before them,
like the vanguard of the little fleet,
their new-born daughter in the ribboned carriage,
shiny tiny golden earrings already in her ears.

Across the way,
a white-smocked youngster cries his wares,
the tray of *barquillos* he would sell
carefully balanced on his head,
the tray of wares so carefully covered with the
        flimsiest nettings,
you'd think them made of moths
which had folded up their wings against the
        the day of sun;
and the children's eyes appraise
the thin vanilla wafers
rolled to shapes of honey-colored cornucopias,
as again he cries, *"Barquillos."*

And so fresh and sharp, this family group,
as it sails and flows along the streams of shade,
a part of the parade, yet separate and complete
in its perfect composition,
spun in sun and carved by lights and darks,
it is like a moving tableau made of paper, plaster,
iced and frosted, put together by a decorator
to be set in some store window near the park,
selling new white suits,
or organdies,
baby carriages,
— or Sundays.

YOU GO ABROAD TO FIND YOURSELF

You go abroad to find yourself,
and if not totally unreceptive,
you learn what you would have known
    all along
at home
had you been a bit more perceptive;
for in traveling one confirms
the answer given years ago,
and never really heard
until now.

ALONG THE NORTH CANTABRIAN SEA

Cloud shadows counterpoint
the darks and lights of hills and valleys
as if to hold them in an over-all design,
equivocate the picture plane;
and then, framed from within the eye,
reduced to a wieldy size,
say a 3½ by 5,
the scene becomes the view,
held in such a visual grasp it can't be lost,
a fluid moment in a sort of stasis,
complete and separate from the others,
saved still;
and so it comes to be
not the post card chosen,
mailed home to keep for sure,
sent to several friends,
but no, a panorama personally ours,
the high point and epitome, itself become
    the counterpoint
to all the other ohs and ahs
seen through the window of the bus
which carried us
across Northwestern Spain
along the Cantabrian Sea.

TEDIUM IN THE TROPICS

Fringy thumbs of palm trees
waggle at you from the horizon line,
as if, bored with the view,
they would hitch a ride with you,
not knowing you're stuck, too.

IN SPAIN, THE SIESTA

In Spain, with days of sun to spare,
how welcome the siesta;
here, at home,
one wallows in the noon,
not counting on the after.

IN THE PALACE OF THE DUKE OF ALBA

Marguerites climb the beech,
and roses climb the marble pillars;
and in the patio in the corners,
palm trees stand with great aplomb
and watch, one supposes, from time
to time the Duke of Alba
climb the wide and curving staircase
from the courtyard to his quarters.

THE PEDESTRIAN SWING

I must say, my dear,
you write with a very pedestrian swing;
well, being a walker, how can I help it
getting the rhythm into my brain.

IT WAS THE MAUVEST SUNSET

It was the mauvest sunset,
the longest and the largest one I ever saw,
filling the bay as well as the sky,
the window the wall as well as my eye,
till I took it in through violet skin,
the aura of mauveness becoming my being;
and black Lab Rock an island himself
was dreaming in clouds of lilac.

Now the lights coming on at the new Marina
are cubing the moorings, the docks, the piers,
the boats and floats, the shops, the ways, and
        all kinds of gear
to a village alone,
limned, shot through and traced in lights
to an almost brittle brilliance,
a kind of chartreuse magic wonder
as if to counter the violet spell
pressing, diffusing its essence,
and the sky leaning toward us a toppling wall.

And the honey-comb village, wound up
in a strangle of green aureolin yellow,
floating in a sea of its own transcendence,
relieves the eye but not for long,
as we remember the fluorescence will in the end
make tenser, not only itself,
but the mauveness increasing, pervading the night,
come to enclose us invade us and finally take all.

ON THE FERRY FROM COLUMBIA BEACH
TO MUKILTEO

It was as if the bay had transferred its wetness to the hills,
conferred limpidity at last
on the houses, yards, and lights of Mukilteo;
not at all as if all were run with water in a winter storm,
but no, set out lovingly by a summer evening newly come,
enmeshing in its softness
the velvet lawns with the velvet of the night and bay,
with the voluminous folds of hills
half asleep
like benevolent well-fed mystics
arms akimbo
bestowing princely ruminations on the hour
regarding such and such and all, in all relationships,
until there was an unsharp lucidity to the whole,
until the evergreen dark pockets hollowing out the contours
might even be the undersides of waves awash;
and as for the ferry lights, where are they,
aboard, ashore, or in my eyes?

SHE LOOKED AT THE BAY

She looked at the bay as if to draw sustenance
        from that,
forgetting for the moment
the bitter salt
the rank kelp
and the changing currents even there.

17

THE BRAND NEW FREIGHTER JUST COME IN

A panoply of white superstructure
caped by the Olympic Mountains canopy,
white as snow, fresh as paint,
makes one wonder at the spars and masts.
Are they frozen here at Pier I,
or over there across the bay
against the glaciered ridges,
caverned now to even deeper fissures,
by side-long thrusts of sun;
and say, who let the paint bucket
roll and splash and fall away
among, upon those mountains there,
and around the packages of two-by-twelves
ready to be hoisted from the city pier.

This thing one sees, on a sunny morning,
looking down from town
at the brand new freighter just come in
to take on lumber here.

SO WINDY THE WHITE CAPS SEEM REAL

So windy the white caps seem real,
so blue the sky might break
if the clouds sailing by get too close for
    safety's sake;
and the daffodils,
petals stiff with plastic yellow,
seem to talk in hurried fits of chats
as they lean over
on rubbery legs of stalks,
heads together,
as if to duck the shotgun blasts of weather.

THE BAY CALM WITH SUCH APLOMB

Cloud shapes repeat themselves below
in flat drifts of snow; and sailboats, barges,
shine the bay's surface, would dent it, too,
sailing, plowing through. But the water skin
resists the taking over, and, with no
show of panic, bends the masts to right
angles, indeed, defends itself with such
a force of fierceness, as well as subtly conceived
finangles, as to throw the boat and barge
shapes back at the aggressors; in fact,
creates such havoc with the bay traffic,
despite the largeness of the stillness, blocking
entrances with extra warehouses, doubling
piers, twisting pilings to horizontal
crooked fences, even the floats of snow
floes, riding their survival, are very
incidental facets of the reflections
which collide, elide, penetrate
and slide, interlaced with interweaving
layers of design; although the surface
of the water counters this with such aplomb,
one looks long from the window, thinking, my,
how calm the bay is, what a limpid day
it is, hardly a breath of air stirring.
No, not much going on out there this morning.

A SNOWIE DAY

Good for sights out the window
and slips on the sidewalk;
and evergreens weary from their loads,
once released, swing like blind boxers
in a battle with the wind;
all they fight for, we know, is their status quo,
but what a whirligig go-round flailing
to regain their regal bearing,
retain their right to stand with appropriate mien
in their accustomed places,
surely theirs by right of having been there
through all kinds of weather,
and their survival of this last inclemency
must give them extra claims to tenancy.

IT WAS THE QUIETEST FOURTH

It was the quietest Fourth.
The mills quit blowing their stacks.
The kids gone to the beach
to snap their pistol caps.
And the fireworks not on
till ten o'clock tonight.

It was the quietest Fourth.
A neighbor calls and asks,
"Can I fly my flag, d'you think?
With only 48 stars?"
"Well yes why not," I told her,
and turned to write a letter.

But the keys I struck made such
a staccato stiletto sound,
such a hollow brittle one,
I stopped to take a nap.
And then the day came whole again
on a Fourth I will remember.

REMEMBER THE DAY THE WIND CAME OUT?

(for Si and Bri)

Remember the day the wind came out?
And we tried to go for a ride
and hit the lawn instead?
Oh the wind would give us a fly all right,
the afternoon of the Fourth of July,
and off we sailed from the top of the front porch railing,
umbrellas held high to catch the breeze.
O, we would give it a try.

How we leaped for the wind to float us on up,
at least to catch us a cloud
to sustain us up there in our made-up world,
only to learn that up could be down
when we came back to earth in a series of bumps,
just missing the flower garden.

And the grumpy grown-ups,
aware of perils of such levitation,
alarmed at our faith in ourselves and umbrellas,
demanded we abandon veranda games
for something more grand,
like the Fourth of July pyrotechnic display
about to come up, or down,
depending on where we would be.

For there *must* be a way to catch onto clouds,
umbrellas clutched tight and wide open enough
to get us up off of the porch,
and then, having proved our flight okay,
we wouldn't be here, but *there,*
watching the rockets soar with ohs and ahs
as they rose to bloom then fall toward the bay;
and our families and friends on top of the garage,
shuffling their chairs, smoking cigars,
and passing the opera glasses with huzzas,
    hurrahs, and hoorays;
yes, we would waive the watermelon waiting,
the ice cream made in the ice cream trays of the
    new frigidaire.

We would trade all this
for the other side of the gunpowder flowers,
to watch umbrella-shaped clusters of lightning-quick petals
rise to us in the glare, twinkle and go,
disappear and fall in the wilt and tilt of a second
and flares all around us as real as street lamps and stars.
Wow, what a view!

And true!
And so real can't you still see it now?
Though we never did get to the sky, of course,
having had to stay below with people, grumpy,
knowing they will never know more than they know,
    and why,
because no one believes in miracles
except for kids who want to fly.
And no one but us believed in the wind
the day it came out that Fourth of July.

COMMENCEMENT, 1966

502 high school seniors
sit row on evenly receding row
on the auditorium platform,
and as they listen,
their tasseled mortar boards
lightly turn in a kind of unison,
like petals lowering, swaying,
as if each, breathing with the breath of the wearer,
bearer of the blue and gold of EHS,
is in time with a rhythm stronger than its own;
and the homogeneous mass of the face of the
      Class of 1966,
with just the slightest tremble,
keeps breaking into a great gigantic flower,
a flat, blue and gold trapezium-shaped chrysanthemum.

502 high school graduates
rise now, row by even row,
and break the composition
as they move forward, row by row, right of center,
where the principal reads the names,
and a school board member gives out the diplomas.

Each waits his turn,
then walks alone
in cap and gown
across the stage,
posture good,
step assured.
Applause is reserved for the line in total.

Where is it they are going?
Do they know?
They should.

The principal, superintendent, school board member,
and three class speakers
have told them the line of march lies forward,
the future looking fine,
with one or two slight reservations;
and if higher education is not for all,
there are still the Elysian Fields of further contemplation,
and the joys of realizing life's potential.

Meanwhile,
parents, families, sidereal relations
applaud the goings-on, in turn;
and shot-off flashbulbs
echo back and forth across the auditorium,
though cameras with distracting lights are forbidden.

Now the lines form again,
and it is over.

The graduates en masse
rush up the aisle
to the tune of Pomp and Circumstance;
and as they crowd the çorridors,
faces in the balcony swell like balloons
and are surely going to burst
as they smile and twist
to watch the Class of '66 take off
for the land of compromise,
chance and happenstance,
yes and no, maybe and perhaps.

But first the out-of-school-at-last celebration,
the   one-night hiatus between commencement
    and departure,
the all-night dance at the Elks,
with fortune-telling booths besides the band;
and games of black jack, roulette, craps
so set up they can't get out of hand,
and no one really loses,
since the stakes are fake,
and the croupiers, their parents. .

So which way the ball is going to bounce,
or how the cards will fall,
isn't going to matter much,
no, not just this once;
and the difference is,
the participants,
no longer students, still,
are graduates who don't quite know it yet,
and won't,
until tomorrow.

SATURDAY NIGHT AT FLETCHER'S BAY

O the scrape of the feet on the dance floor
in time with the tune,
the couple scissoring its scraping way
to rhythms of the saxophone,
the trumpet, and the sweet piano
in cacophonies of its own;
and whispering how they whisper scissor
round the corner back again,
streaming with the ever-so-slight jostling,
a part of yet separate from
summer friends and Islanders
going round around the main-go-round
in the old barn of a dance hall on the Island.

How they beat out the time
with sliding gliding steps peculiar to
    themselves alone,
yet in rhyme with the slightly swaying pattern
of the nearly-touching ever-continuing
    almost-silent throng,
as if the band on the platform, in full command,
had become their puppeteers,
manipulating them to slightly straying swaying puppets
loosely held, yet clearly all in hand.

And the tuba player on the floor
is in and out and through the crowd,
his rotund shape so like the oompah bah
and bellow of the horn;

and now the dancers streaming by
are streaming in a dream stronger than they know,
led by the sweet piano
yet leading more and more,
and even the drums and traps are letting go.

For the throng of puppets are puppets getting
    out of hand,
and it seems they are about to seize the puppet strings
and soon will lead the band.
And the band cannot shake loose
and must play faster, faster
keeping pace.

And the instant spins into one hundred
    simultaneous seconds,
into such a whirl, a tension calming building up,
a silence ready to explode
a scene in and out of balance,
you'd think the rising vortex
a tornado built of music
about to twist the roof and windows off.

But then, just in time, intermission time.
Eleven o'clock.
And the splittering second whirls, whorls,
    comes whole again,
and with a flourish and a run, the band
    suspends its playing,
and the dancers stop because they can and must,
loosed as they are at last from the circle's grasp,
and the ladies club is setting out the evening lunch.

And the couple is relieved, almost, to have it ended,
having latched on to something stronger
    than intended,
something building to a mounting force so
    intense complex,
it was about to take them over and would
    have run the show.

And if the intermission had not come to save them,
the dancers would have danced gyrated till the end,
yes, they would have disappeared
into a hundred disparate jets of separating colors,
each a solitary messenger
with a single message audible to all,
yet no one really hearing, caring, listening, evanescing,
no, not even the one now remembering,
slowly walking to the bench alongside the wall,
the dance hall back in focus now,
and thanks for the dance he was saying,
and well thank you was all she answered him.

ALL AND NOTHING IN SUSPENSE

How futile and intense it was.
Once begun,
it commenced the see-saw zig-zag push and pull
and then with such a surface roar
evaporated all at once
and that's the way one feels growing up,
immense,
and all and nothing in suspense.

REMEMBER THE MOVIE STARS

Remember the movie stars
who came with the chocolate bars
we bought at the store by the school;
where, if you bit into a colored mint,
you got five more;
the fake cigarettes and the chocolate eclairs,
and cups of chocolate
steaming hot for Sunday tea;
then the real cigarettes
we smoked occasionally
deep in the ravine damp with maiden hair
and bracken three feet tall;
and even later on, the cabin,
the alder fire recalling all;
and how we wondered then
what it was would bring us five and get us ten,
and how the mint would taste again,
colored pink or yellow-green;
and where to go and who to see;
and what had happened to the movie stars
we had collected so assidiously.

I KNEW A STORM WAS BREWING

At first I thought it was a plane overhead,
and then a train coming,
but when I saw the branches bowing, swaying,
heard them battering on the window
like waves moving in,
then I knew a storm was brewing, blowing up,
and sure enough, here it was
rip-snorting right around the corner
like it was the first great wind ever
off the bay;
and it is late, nearly dusk,
and all is grey, grey all over
and the grey thing coming
batters at the house till I know it will be covered
in flecks of grey,
a kind of warm grey fur
hanging from and wrapping round the porches,
a good thing perhaps,
for this old house needs steadying on its perches,
on its haunches so close
to the bluff;
but even so,
long before the wind is going to finish with itself,
this one inside the house has had enough,
as has the dog, as has the house,
as has this fistful of grey stuff,
this squeezed out fistful of what started out as
    grey warm fluff,
blown to bits then squeezed to this,
a wet lump of almost nothing soggy grey in my fist.

THE RAIN WAS A LONG TIME COMING

For hours the storm was brewing;
and the rain was a long time coming.
You could smell the rain in the breezes unevenly increasing
and you could hear the storm in the swaying of the trees.
Leaves scuttled along the roof gutters,
doors and windows creaked,
and even the shutters began to bang against the house.

All day long you watched the waves in frets of push and pulls
pile up against the log booms,
impede paths of tugs,
splash across the jetty;
and mill stack smoke leaning Westward
throw handfuls of semi-transparent flowers
flatter and further out over the bay away from town.

Undecided seagulls completely lost their poise
and lumbered back and forth,
plump with worry,
like ambulatory bundles of laundry
abandoned on the back lawn.
And the wet air had begun to taste more and more of salt.

Then, along towards evening, the storm broke.
And for all the build-up, was a weak one.
The rain stayed on no longer than that,
and left you wondering how it could have taken so long coming
when it had so little to say.

And as for the wind, what a noise and a rattle
            and rumble it made,
blowing and blowing right up to the crux,
and then all at once,
as if tired of the fuss,
blew off the storm
and stumbled away to be by itself.

WHATEVER ELSE IT IS ONE KNOWS

And now begins again the long slow walk of winter,
and I am walking home
in the half-rains half-darks of November,
thinking how the house lights coming on,
in half-lights of their own,
make the drabness of the later afternoons
more cozy in a sense though blacker.

And as I walk slowly toward my home alone,
to an aura not forgotten yet,
I think the half-tones of whatever else it is
one knows but somehow can't remember
mean more to me than that.

WITH THE EYES WE HAVE NOW

Just the sight of the half-dried maple leaf
on the lawn outside the window
and I'm back inside the third grade
with our made-up autumn leaves stuck on windows
    walls and doors;
ready for Jack Frost, you know,
and Hallowe'en's slow dog bark in the nippy air;
apples to bob for,
cider to drink
and the squeak-squawk of chalk on the blackboard
spelling the words
for us to see in order to write;
and so it goes,
associations tender, half-brutal, too;
recalling a past we never really knew
and wish we could have seen
with the eyes we have now;
but had that been possible,
perhaps we would not write at all.

THEY SAY

They say your eyes are what you might have been,
your mouth is what you are. Okay.
But it's the gesture, I would say,
tells you true.
The quick hand sweep of the hair,
the driver's handling of the wheel;
and though the gait might yet conceal the limp,
tell me, does the shoulder droop
in any way
disguise the hurt too deep to bear?

THE QUICK GLANCE AND HALF AN EAR

If you would look, make the glance a quick one,
lest the prolonged stare reduce the view;
and to hear a something well,
don't try to hear it all
but let it come up to you,
and then oh then
supply the missing word,
and the meaning ringing clearly in your ear
will tell you what you saw.

THE BOOK MARK FOUND

Were you reading here
the afternoon the door bell rang,
a caller coming for you,
making you break the succeeding line
when you got up to answer,
leaving the book mark marking your place
so you'd know where to come back to?

Were you reading here, I wonder,
in the late afternoon,
not waiting really for anyone to come,
but thinking someone would,
thinking of some long journey soon to take,
when you put down the book
and left the living room?

Was it then she marked her place, I wonder,
leaving it to welcome in the caller at the door,
someone she was expecting,
though not exactly waiting for.

WITH THE SURPRISE ONE HAS

Why,
it is raining out!
And she looked up from the book
with the surprise one has
rousing from a nap
and finding that it's morning.

THE HOME-MADE MYSTIC

The home-made mystic
rubbed 2 sticks,
lit the incense,
let the clouds of blue arise;
and when they hit the sky,
he thought he was experiencing infinity.

So claiming blue as his affinity,
he closed up shop,
took a nap,
and sailed to parts far from this vicinity.

WELL, THEN, WHICH WAY TO TURN

The trouble is,
the dislike of the like,
and the like dislikes the other, too;
well, then, which way to turn
but inward,
and Narcissus-like,
find the pool
worth the stare.

A WALK IN SOFT GREY SMOKES OF TALK

A walk in soft grey smokes of talk;
happy poems, heart-shaped
hang from trees;
o tell us trees,
trellis trees,
let us trees hear your words of leaves;
opened up like palms
stretching toward us,
yes, let us shake your hands
establish our rapport;
yes, let us walk among the trees
with wisps of smoke hair in their leaves
let us listen to the lisp
of almost-told stories.

Bookworm & Silverfish Box 639, Wytheville, VA 24382

Ph: (276) 686-5813 | Fax: (276) 686-6636

5687055807

2C-6

(Poetry)
(Poetry) Duryee, Marjorie. THE IMAGE COLLECTOR VII. Portland, 1967, 56pp. First ed. Vg in a yellow base dust jacket that shows some soil. Unclipt.

WYY

$15.00

SOMETIMES THE DREAM DIES HARD

Sometimes the dream dies hard,
not with a crackle and a pop,
not with a slow and slushy sigh,
but a little and a little drops away,
as if the heart had opened up a bit,
just in time to say goodbye.

IF THERE'S ANYTHING HAS A HOLLOW RING

If there's anything has a hollow ring
it's the unanswered telephone bell
ringing for the tenth time,
echoing the empty hall and empty room
and the mindless one staring there not answering.

BECAUSE THERE WAS SO LITTLE TIME

Because there was so little time,
they cast aside the unimportant,
yet spoke of little else;
the moral being I suppose,
more or less,
one can't compress a life
to an afternoon's conversation;
and who tries,
loses even more than this.

IF YOU CAN'T SEE IT?

If you can't see it,
how can it be there?
and without a label,
is it real?

PERSISTENT FANTASY

Oh why do I wake up dreaming you are here,
when I fling you from me every night?
Oh why do I wake to hear your voice call out
when I've torn it from me and thrown it to the fire;
oh why do I lie sleeping on your shoulder
when it's the worn-out couch my head is on,
and the arms around me the morning of grey November.

WHAT IS MEMORY BUT A SERIES OF
DISTORTED IMAGES?

The studio easels,
with their various planes of canvas,
twist the model through the room.

Mirrors of distortion,
they are the pictures
which step across your eyes
as you sit before the fire
trying to piece together
the total mind.

A POUSSE-CAFÉ OF METAPHORS

Might as well accept the weather;
collect the rusted iron and metal;
and let the colors run,
russet green chrome and yellow
till you have before you
a pousse-café of metaphors.

No need to sip as there is more,
but too great a swallow
and you will drown in what you know,
though the glass be shallow.

GETTING OVER THE FLU

Trouble is, there's too much time to think,
not steam enough to do;
and so the grass has grown two feet high,
and so your world has shrunk to one good eye,
and so your space is half a window without a shade,
and so you lie arrested
in the bed you haven't made.

ONE THINKS HOW GREAT IT WOULD BE

One thinks how great it would be
cutting loose, being free;
but then, having been,
I am remembering
how the world follows on
wherever one would go,
for there is nothing really new
at least in the one we know;
and as for the other one,
the mother yet to come,
the question stays to sting:
will we recognize the new, the changing thing,
or count it just another spring?

NOTE TO ONESELF

(to clean out the house)

Can hardly see the sky,
so smash the trash,
bash it,
else it cover you completely
forever hide the view.
So you do.
And then so busy picking up the pieces you have smashed,
wondering why,
still no time to see the sky,
or watch the mountain peaks coming through,
which they are,
right at you!

44

WON'T YOU COME TO DINNER?

Now nothing controversial
no talk of sex or politics
religion or relinquishment,
or unrequited love.
No, nothing negative.

Yes, keep the conversation happy,
be aware of what you're talking of;
make it cute and make it snappy
and for heaven's sake don't get intense;

no, cut out the arguments,
be neither hawk nor dove;
just ride the fence
with your hands in your pockets
and your heart full of,
well, I don't know,
just so long as it doesn't throw you off.

LIKE THE WAY I SOMETIMES THINK

Rocky, I'm *not* getting up to let you out,
and all the time I'm saying this
I'm getting up to let him out and why?
Because he sits and stares at me with eyes that never blink.
Scares me, it's so like the way I sometimes think.

CONCERNING THE GREEN TURTLE, SEE
RHETORICAL QUESTIONS

Must we go through life reading the travel folders
to know where we have been,
where we would like to go;
and buy the picture post cards
to confirm the view of what we've seen,
and what is so?

And when the little boy next door
with his green umbrella
claims he's not a toadstool but a turtle,
must we check the index first, page and title,
before we will admit
the little guy is right
and yes, his umbrella makes a good turtle shell
as any toadstool will be glad to tell you.

TO ALL THE AFTERNOONS OF MOMENTS SUCH
AS THESE

To all the little moments
like little drops of rain
almost alike not quite the same
in shape or size
in place in space
in time in mind;
to all these little moments let me say
I salute you
for your constancy
as consistent as the rain patina on the window pane
a rhythmic chiming pattern
at once alive and here and gone
yet staying on
through all the afternoons of moments such as these.

BLOOMED RHODODENDRONS

Spider-like skeletons
of bloomed rhododendrons
take giant steps
on stem ends;
march in place.

Seems a thousand of them
go which way at once
round the old bush;
clusters of walking arrangements
on half-bent legs.

Remnants of blossoms, yes;
spidery stables, maybe;
or revenants of arachnid insects, perhaps,
I can't help thinking
as I remove them.

stabiLES

HAVING TO DO WITH SPRINKLERS ON THE LAWN

Rock enjoys his showers
all summer long,
tries all the sprinklers set
to whirling bowing combing sprayings
up and down and across the lawn
till he finds his favorite,
a zingaling whirligig go-round,
tests it with a leg,
tastes the water biting it,
backs up to it with his tail,
and then sits softly, safely from the center,
lets the made-up rain batter
his black coat.

Then, enough,
comes on the porch
to shrug it off
as if to say,
see, I'll share my bath with you,
you want to cool off too don't you?

No I don't
but what to do,
admit the day has gone long since
when in wet cotton clinging bathing suits
we ran through sprinklers on the lawn,
different sizes, shapes, and circles then,
but even so
what beautiful angel wings we made
just for seconds
spreading our wet arms
on the sidewalk going round the house,
the abrasiveness of the rough and hot cement
such a delight of counter-feeling to the
    goose flesh bumps
as we lay shivering.

SUCH A SHINY THING

Such a shiny thing.
So tiny, thin, and shimmering.
What motivates its being?
The iridescence of its wings?
Or is this an echo of the eye?
An answer to the yes perhaps,
the breathing in of a world I know,
the landscape of my pulse.

How I stare, wondering
if this rapport is only chance
between the here and now and there.
Or if I am seeing, say,
just a tiny being, shimmering,
as separate as a day
from somewhere far away
come to stay a shiny green thing.

THE MAPLE TREES

The maple trees
growing from the ravine,
with fronds like jungle palms of some kind,
reach out their multiple hands
as if to feel another being,
as dense and green,
walking along the street
in the amost-indigo of evening.

THE DAY YOU LEFT

The day you left
it rained a deep ironic grey;
deep because so like your eyes I felt so blue;
ironic for in almost knowing you I doubly
    lost you, too;
and grey because you did not stay.
All three of these combined,
the day you went away,
to take my mind;
for the going,
be it man or time,
takes something from the one who's left behind,
to contemplate the rain.

Yes, the rain the rain,
the truest friend the radio,
the weather on the hour,
gusty winds sure to blow and showers certain,
soon to come and none to go,
and chances are a hundred per cent
the one who went will not be back,
no no no;
and being as how it's now ten after ten,
weather due again at eleven,
chances are there'll be no changes made,
no, not even then.

THE TOAD LET GO

Having hoed an unexpected toad
as I was cultivating, barefoot,
a row of tomato plants
in someone else's garden,
I held the bulbous half-round stone,
yes, so lean the hips, so full the chest,
clammy cold between my toes;
and then reluctantly let go
this almost-alive thing
into the rich brown earth,
all the while wondering
how, so ponderous in shape,
and despite the chill it brought,
it could have come so pulsing.

And still I thought, standing there,
was it not worth the keeping,
this simulated toad let go
back into the real live growing garden,
long since plowed through, of course,
and turned to grass,
the only thing to last,
for a while at least,
a half-round stone held close
between my toes,
and then let go beneath my feet,
but not my notice.

No, and yes,
a stone so like the toad I one time found and cherished,
or a bull frog, all the same to us,
the toad I tried so hard to catch,
and finally did,
and brought him home
to keep safe and warm in the basement laundry tub.

And though I was not aware of the nuisance of the croaking,
the danger from his warts,
others were, I guess,
for when we went to spend the weekend in Seattle,
to visit my grandmother,
the maid turned loose my amphibious pet,
with the slightest implication left
that the stalwart toad, to wit, had freed itself..

And I can see him yet,
skedaddling down the alley,
then limping just a bit,
as tired toads do,
from leaping cracks in the cement
and from being wary of sticky patches of tar
so ready to get him stuck;
and finally then with a huff and a puff,
surmounting moats of ditches filled with water
and home again, triumphant, in the frog pond at
    the corner,
at the bottom of the drive;

home again to his castle in the swampy leaves,
and safe from dogs and cats, rabbits in their hutches,
garter snakes in grocery boxes,
trucks and ordinary walkers,
and stalks of coarse quack grass which would cut him
    to the quick.
And there he resumed his role as master
of all the other toads, frogs, and tadpoles
alive on Rucker Hill.

The pool is filled in now,
a white colonial house standing there;
and the only toads you hear
are the few who disappear, anonymous,
to do their careful croaking
in the bushes high and dry nearby;
discreet cries, and a far cry
from the generations past who congregated at the pool,
in full view,
to flex their leg muscles,
show off their warty backs,
and bellow from their lungs, so large and under-slung;

and practice, how they practiced,
their melodious tunes, hardly under-sung,
accompanying our after-dinner games
in The Grove at the corner,
Punch the Grapes, Run Sheep Run,
and The Sheik of Arabeek
played on the victrola.

And the biggest one of all, the daddy toad, my pet,
would swell and swell and swell
until you'd swear his mighty chest was going to burst;
but no, he would breathe the warm evening air
into the loveliest croaks of all;
and you could feel their roundingness
as they rose one by one to the limpid sky.

And there they hung,
and you could almost hear them say,
in their suspension, and growing nothingness,
caroak goodbye caroak goodbye
goodbye caroak goodbye caroak
let go caroak so long caroak let go caroak goodbye.